How to Use this Book

Matched to the National Curriculum, this Collins Year 1 Reading Comprehension workbook is designed to improve comprehension skills.

Diverse and engaging texts including **fiction**, **non-fiction** and **poetry**.

Tests **increase in difficulty** as you work through the book.

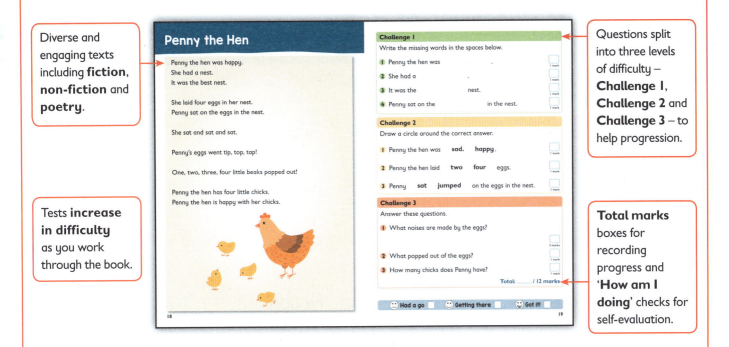

Questions split into three levels of difficulty – **Challenge 1**, **Challenge 2** and **Challenge 3** – to help progression.

Total marks boxes for recording progress and '**How am I doing**' checks for self-evaluation.

Starter test recaps skills covered in reception.

Three **Progress tests** included throughout the book for ongoing assessment and monitoring progress.

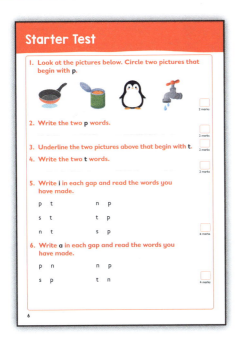

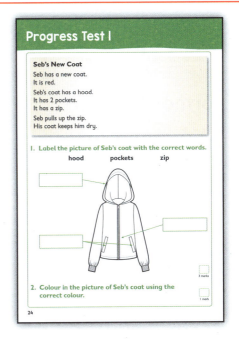

Answers provided for all the questions.

Contents

Acknowledgments

The author and publisher are grateful to the copyright holders for permission to use quoted materials and images.

'My Old Teddy' by Dom Mansell was published by Walker Books. © Dom Mansell, 1991.

All illustrations and images are ©Shutterstock.com and ©HarperCollinsPublishers Ltd.

Published by Collins
An imprint of HarperCollins*Publishers*
1 London Bridge Street
London SE1 9GF

HarperCollins*Publishers*
Macken House, 39/40 Mayor Street Upper,
Dublin 1, D01 C9W8, Ireland

© HarperCollins*Publishers* Limited 2021

ISBN 978-0-00-846755-5

First published 2021

10 9 8 7 6 5 4 3 2

British Library Cataloguing in Publication Data.

A CIP record of this book is available from the British Library.

Publisher: Fiona McGlade
Author: Rachel Clarke
Copyeditor: Fiona Watson
Project Management: Shelley Teasdale
Cover Design: Sarah Duxbury
Inside Concept Design and Page Layout: Ian Wrigley
Production: Karen Nulty
Printed in India by Multivista Global Pvt. Ltd.

MIX
Paper | Supporting
responsible forestry
FSC™ C007454

This book is produced from independently certified FSC™ paper to ensure responsible forest management.

For more information visit:
www.harpercollins.co.uk/green

Reading Comprehension at Home

These ideas for games and activities can be easily carried out at home when reading for pleasure with your child, or when your child is reading for pleasure on their own. They will help build your child's comprehension skills and are fun to do.

Sing nursery rhymes

Nursery rhymes are a good way for children to learn about rhythm, rhyme and pattern. Lots of nursery rhymes are mini stories with beginnings, middles and ends, and different characters and settings, just like longer stories. Nursery rhymes also introduce children to older and more unusual words that they might otherwise not come across.

Share wordless picture books

Wordless picture books are excellent for encouraging children to tell their own stories based on the illustrations. Take turns with your child to tell a story using a wordless picture book. It's good fun to use character voices and to change the way you read (quickly, slowly, quietly, loudly, etc.) to reflect the meaning in the illustrations.

Make puppets

Making puppets to help retell a story is great fun too. You can make puppets from clothes pegs, wooden spoons, old socks and pieces of card stuck to lollipop sticks. Retelling a story in this way helps your child remember the sequence of events and to begin to think about the thoughts and feelings of different characters.

Read aloud

Reading aloud is one of the best ways to encourage your child to develop a love of reading. Try to make time to read aloud to your child every day. This can be from a storybook, a poem or an information book. Make the reading as pleasurable as you can, maybe by sharing a drink or treat together, or by cuddling up as you read.

Make connections

When you are reading with your child, encourage them to make connections between the book and their own experiences. For example, you may want to ask them if they remember a time when they had a similar experience to a character in the book; if they can think of other poems with similar characters, settings or themes; or if they've seen or heard about the information you read in a non-fiction book.

Word families

When you are reading with your child, take the time to explore the meaning of unfamiliar words, to ensure they understand what they have read. Encourage them to use the context to help them to work out what new words mean, but don't be afraid to use a dictionary to check the meaning. Collect words your child is familiar with and which have similar meanings to develop their understanding.

Picture perfect

When you are reading non-fiction with your child, consider the pictures and diagrams that have been included, as well as the words. Discuss why those particular pictures or diagrams might have been chosen, and how they help the reader to understand the text. Ask your child to suggest other pictures and diagrams they would like to see included on the page.

Join the library

Borrowing books from your local library is an easy and inexpensive way to ensure that your child experiences a wide range of books. Children's librarians are experts at ensuring their collections are full of well-loved classics, new releases, comics, audio stories and interesting non-fiction. Many local libraries also run story sessions and arrange activity sessions aimed at encouraging reading.

Starter Test

1. **Look at the pictures below. Circle two pictures that begin with p.**

 2
2 marks

2. **Write the two p words.**

 Pengben   Pan

2
2 marks

3. **Underline the two pictures above that begin with t.**

2
2 marks

4. **Write the two t words.**

tin   tap

 2
2 marks

5. **Write i in each gap and read the words you have made.**

p i t   n i p

s i t   t i p

n i t   s i p

 6
6 marks

6. **Write a in each gap and read the words you have made.**

p a n   n a p

s a p   t a n

 4
4 marks

7. These pictures tell the story of Hickory Dickory Dock but they have been put in the wrong order. Put the pictures in the right order using the numbers 1 to 3.

2   1   3

3

3 marks

8. Write **ck** in each gap and read the words you have made.

ti C K   to C K   pa C K   ki C K   so C K

clo C K   qua C K   do C K   chi C K   ba C K

10

10 marks

9. Write the correct word in each gap. Ask an adult to help you read the story of Hickory Dickory Dock.

Hickory Dickory _dock_ ,

The mouse ran up the _clock_ .

The clock struck one,

The mouse ran _down_ !

Hickory Dickory _tick tock_ .

3

4 marks

10. Read these words and point to them on the picture.

ball      sand   tree

bucket   starfish   beach   ring

8 marks

11. Circle three words above that begin with s.

3 marks

12. Underline three words above that begin with b.

3 marks

13. Tick to show the correct answers.

The children are at the   **beach.** ✓   **park.** ✗

There are   **four children.** ✗   **six children.** ✓

The children have   **three buckets.** ✗   **two buckets.** ✓

The starfish is   **on the sand.** ✓   **in the sea.** ✗

The ball is   **on the sand.** ✗   **in the sea.** ✓

5 marks

14. Read these words.

duck   cat   dog   hen   bee   cow

15. Write the name of each animal on the lines.

hen

duck

cat

dog

cow

Bee

16. These sentences are about each of the animals but the words have been put in the wrong order. Write each sentence in the right order.

moo! Cows go   *Cows go moo ʃ*

laid an egg. The hen

a long tail. The dog has

17. **These pictures tell the story of Jack and Jill but they have been put in the wrong order. Put the pictures in the right order using the numbers 1 to 4.**

4

4 marks

18. **Write ll in each gap and read the words you have made.**

Ji l l   hi l l   fe l l   we l l

4

4 marks

19. **Write the correct word in each gap. Ask an adult to help you read the story of Jack and Jill.**

Jack and ＿＿＿＿ went up the ＿＿＿＿ to fetch a pail of water.

Jack ＿＿＿＿ down and broke his crown and Jill came tumbling after.

3

3 marks

20. **Write ow in each gap and read the words you have made.**

d o w n   cr o w n   o w l   n o w

4

4 marks

21. Read these words and point to them on the picture.

car   book   rug   teddy   hat

5 marks

22. Tick to show the correct answers.

The children are **at school.** ✓   **at the zoo.** ✗

There are **eight children.** ✓   **six children.** ✗

The teacher is **on the box.** ✗   **on the stool.** ✓

A ball is **in the box.** ✓   **on the rug.** ✗

5 marks

23. Write the missing words in the sentences.

The teacher is reading a ___book___ .

Two children are playing with the ___Blocks.___ A+ .

A boy is wearing a ___hat___ .

3 marks

Total: _____ / 97 marks

Rocket to the Moon

Nadeem got a box.

He put a rug and a mug in it.

He put a pink bun in it.

He put his teddy in it.

was

He put on his boots and his hat.

He got in his rocket. Whoosh!

The rocket went up, up, up.

It went higher and higher and higher.

Zoom! Zoom! Zoom!

Bang! Nadeem was on the moon.

He got out of the rocket.

He got out the rug and the mug.

He got out the pink bun.

He got out his teddy and had a picnic on the moon.

Nadeem got into the rocket with the mug
and the rug and his teddy.

Whoosh! They went down, down, down.

Zoom! Zoom! Zoom!

Bang! Nadeem and teddy were back.

Nadeem got out of the box and put it away.

Challenge 1

1. Write the name of each item on the lines. Use the story to help you spell the words.

Box   Teddy   moon   shoes

4
4 marks

Challenge 2

Add the missing words to the sentences. Use the story to help you spell the words.

1. He put a _____rug_____ and a mug in it.

1
1 mark

2. It went higher and _____higher_____ and higher.

1
1 mark

3. He got out his _____teddy_____ and had a _____picnic_____ on the moon.

2
2 marks

4. Nadeem got out of the _____box_____ and put it away.

1
1 mark

Challenge 3

Answer these questions. Use the story to help you spell the words.

1. What did Nadeem turn the box into? _____rocket_____

1
1 mark

2. What did Nadeem eat for his picnic? _____pink bun_____

1
1 mark

3. What did Nadeem do with the box when he got back? _____He put it away_____

1
1 mark

4. Where would you go if you made a rocket? the hmooh

1
1 mark

Total: ___13___ / 13 marks

😐 Had a go ☐   🙂 Getting there ☐   😃 Got it! ✓

13

Foxes

This is a baby **fox**.
He is called a **cub**.

This is his mummy.
She is called a **vixen**.
She has a red coat and a bushy tail.
She has a long snout.
She has long legs and pointed ears.

They are red foxes.
They live in a **den**.

They go out at night to find food.
The mummy gets rubbish from bins and finds meat to eat.

They sleep in their den in the day.

Challenge 1

Draw a circle around the correct answer.

1 The baby fox is called a... den (cub) vixen.

1 mark

2 His mummy is called a... den cub (vixen).

1 mark

3 They live in a... (den) cub vixen.

1 mark

Challenge 2

1 Label the picture of the fox with the correct words.

red coat   bushy tail   long snout   long legs   pointed ears

red caat

pointed ears

bushy tail

long snont

long legs

5

5 marks

Challenge 3

Answer these questions.

1 When do foxes go out? _at night_

1 mark

2 Write two things foxes eat. _rubbish and meat_

2

2 marks

3 When do foxes go to sleep? _the day_

1 mark

Total: _12_ **/ 12 marks**

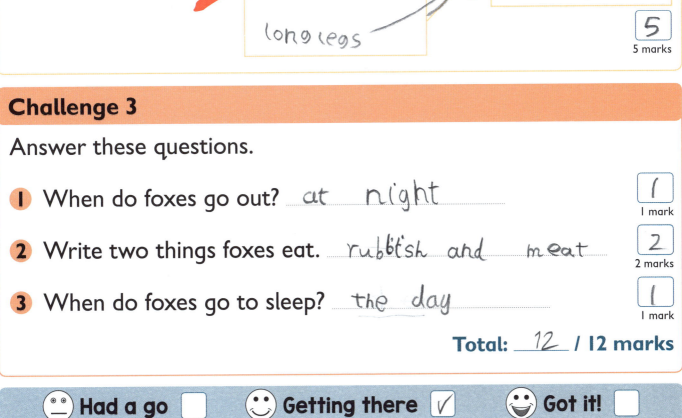

😐 **Had a go** ☐   🙂 **Getting there** ☑   😄 **Got it!** ☐

15

What Can You Hear?

What can you hear at the beach?

I can hear the seagulls screech, screech, screech.

What can you hear at the park?

I can hear the ducks quack, quack, quack.

What can you hear at the shops?

I can hear the tills bleep, bleep, bleep.

What can you hear in the playground?

I can hear the children shout, shout, shout.

What can you hear at the swimming pool?

I can hear the water splash, splash, splash.

What can you hear at the farm?

I can hear the animals moo, baa, oink!

Challenge 1

Tick the correct answer.

1. The girl can hear **seagulls** [✓] **seashells** [✗] at the beach.

1 mark — `(`

2. The girl can hear the tills at **the park.** [✗] **the shops.** [✓]

1 mark — `|`

3. The girl can hear the children at **the playground.** [✓] **the beach.** [✗]

1 mark — `|`

4. The girl can hear **tractors** [✗] **animals** [✓] at the farm.

1 mark — `|`

Challenge 2

Answer these questions.

1. What sound do the seagulls make? ___screech___

1 mark — `(`

2. Where does the girl hear the ducks? ___park___

1 mark — `(`

3. Where does the girl hear splash, splash, splash?

___Swimming pool___

1 mark — `|`

Challenge 3

1. Draw a circle around the sounds the girl can hear at the farm.

(moo)   quack   screech

(baa)   bleep   (oink)

3 marks — `3`

Total: _____ / 10 marks

😐 **Had a go** [ ]   🙂 **Getting there** [✓]   😃 **Got it!** [ ]

Penny the Hen

Penny the hen was happy.
She had a nest.
It was the best nest.

She laid four eggs in her nest.
Penny sat on the eggs in the nest.

She sat and sat and sat.

Penny's eggs went tip, top, tap!

One, two, three, four little beaks popped out!

Penny the hen has four little chicks.
Penny the hen is happy with her chicks.

Challenge 1

Write the missing words in the spaces below.

1 Penny the hen was _happy_ .

> 1 mark

2 She had a _nest_ .

> 1 mark

3 It was the _best_ nest.

> 1 mark

4 Penny sat on the _nest_ in the nest.

> 1 mark

Challenge 2

Draw a circle around the correct answer.

1 Penny the hen was   sad.   (happy).

> 1 mark

2 Penny the hen laid   **two**   **four**   (eggs.)

> 1 mark

3 Penny   (sat)   **jumped**   (on the eggs in the nest.)

> 1 mark

Challenge 3

Answer these questions.

1 What noises are made by the eggs? ....

....

> 3 marks

2 What popped out of the eggs? ....

> 1 mark

3 How many chicks does Penny have? ....

> 1 mark

Total: _____ / 12 marks

☺ **Had a go** ☐   ☺ **Getting there** ☐   ☺ **Got it!** ✓

19

Ears

We can hear with our ears.
Our ears are small.

Animals can hear with their ears too.

Look at all these ears!

Rabbits' ears are long and thin.

Cats' ears are furry and are
on top of their heads.

Elephants' ears are very big.
They flap them to keep
cool when it is hot.

Frogs' ears are hidden inside their heads.
This is a frog's ear, near its eye.

What a lot of ears!

Challenge 1

1 Write which animal each of these ears belong to.

Elephant   frogs   rabbitts   cat

4 marks

Challenge 2

Tick the correct answer.

1 A frog's ears are **on top of its head.** ✗ inside **its head.** ✓

1 mark

2 A rabbit's ears are **long and thin.** ✓ **small.** ✗

1 mark

3 A cat's ears are **furry.** ✓ **very big.** ✗

1 mark

Challenge 3

Answer these questions.

1 Who has small ears? _frog_

1 mark

2 Why do elephants flap their ears? _to cool down_

1 mark

3 Choose three animals. Write the name of each animal and describe its ears.

2 marks

....

2 marks

....

2 marks

Total: _____ / 15 marks

😐 **Had a go** ☐   🙂 **Getting there** ☐   😃 **Got it!** ☐

I Spy

I spy with my silly eye…

A puffin eating a muffin.

A frog called Mog sitting on a log.

A shaggy yak wearing a yellow mac.

A pair of bears brushing their hair.

A silver fish making a wish.

A dad and a nan washing socks in a pan.

What can you see with your silly eye?

Challenge 1

Write the missing words in the spaces below.

1 A frog called Mog _____ on a log.

☐ 1 mark

2 A shaggy _____ wearing a yellow mac.

☐ 1 mark

3 A silver _____ making a wish.

☐ 1 mark

4 A dad and a nan washing _____ in a pan.

☐ 1 mark

Challenge 2

Write the rhyming words from the poem.

1 | spy | _____

☐ 1 mark

2 | puffin | _____

☐ 1 mark

3 | yak | _____

☐ 1 mark

4 | fish | _____

☐ 1 mark

Challenge 3

Complete these rhyming words.

1 pan   m_____, t_____, v_____

☐ 3 marks

2 hair   f_____, ch_____, st_____

☐ 3 marks

3 log   d_____, f_____, c_____

☐ 3 marks

Total: _____ / 17 marks

☺ **Had a go** ☐   ☺ **Getting there** ☐   ☺ **Got it!** ☐

23

Seb's New Coat

Seb has a new coat.
It is red.

Seb's coat has a hood.
It has 2 pockets.
It has a zip.

Seb pulls up the zip.
His coat keeps him dry.

1. **Label the picture of Seb's coat with the correct words.**

   hood   **pockets**   **zip**

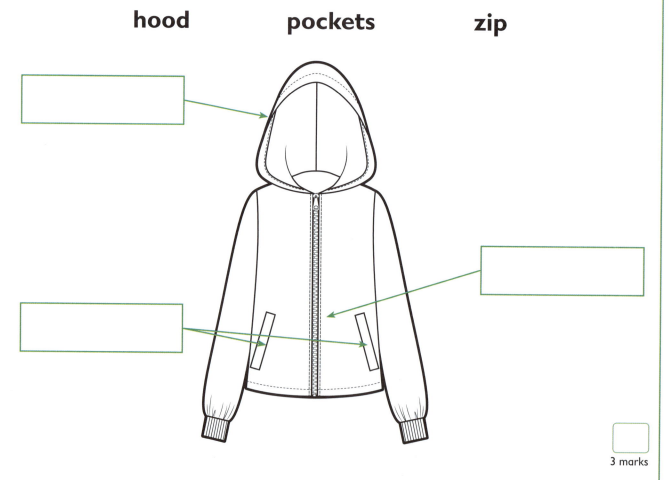

3 marks

2. **Colour in the picture of Seb's coat using the correct colour.**

1 mark

My Dog Rex

My dog is called Rex.

He is a brown dog.

He has big ears and four long legs.

He eats meat.

He eats it fast.

We go to the park with Rex.

He plays with his ball.

He sleeps in a basket.

I love my dog Rex.

Tick the correct answer.

3. **The dog is called**	**Rex.**	☐	**Red.**	☐	1 mark
4. **The dog is**	**black.**	☐	**brown.**	☐	1 mark
5. **The dog's ears are**	**big.**	☐	**small.**	☐	1 mark
6. **The dog eats**	**fish.**	☐	**meat.**	☐	1 mark
7. **The dog plays with a**	**cat.**	☐	**ball.**	☐	1 mark

I'm a Little Teapot

I'm a little teapot,

Short and stout,

Here is my handle,

Here is my spout.

When I get all steamed up,

Hear me shout,

Tip me up and pour me out!

Fill in the gaps in these lines from the poem.

8.   I'm a .... teapot,

1 mark

9.   Here is my .... ,

1 mark

10.   .... is my spout.

1 mark

11.   When I get all .... up,

1 mark

12.   Tip me up and .... me out!

1 mark

Paws

You have feet. Your feet have toes and nails.

Some animals have paws.

Dogs have paws with pads and claws.

Rabbits have paws with sharp claws. They do not have pads.

Cats have sharp claws and soft pads.

Do you know any other animals with paws?

Write answers to these questions.

13. **What do you have on your feet?**

.... **and** ....

2 marks

14. **What do dogs have on their paws?**

.... **and** ....

2 marks

15. **What do rabbits not have on their paws?**

....

1 mark

16. **Which animal has sharp claws and soft pads?**

....

1 mark

Total: _____ / 20 marks

The Enormous Turnip

Long ago, an old woman wanted to cook turnip soup.

She went into the garden to pull up a turnip.
She pulled and pulled but the turnip was stuck.

She asked the old man to help.
He held on to her and they pulled and pulled.
The turnip was stuck.

They got the cow to help.
They all held on and pulled and pulled.
The turnip was still stuck.

Next the dog tried to help.
They all held on and pulled and pulled.
The turnip was stuck.

The cat joined in.
They all held on and pulled and pulled.
The turnip was still stuck.

Then a little mouse came to help.
They all held on and pulled and pulled and pulled.

POP! The turnip came up.
Everyone shouted 'HOORAY!'

The old woman cooked turnip soup for everyone.

Challenge 1

Write the missing words in the spaces below.

1 Long ago, an old woman wanted to _____ turnip soup.

☐ 1 mark

2 She pulled and pulled but the turnip was _____ .

☐ 1 mark

3 He _____ on to her and they pulled and pulled.

☐ 1 mark

4 They _____ the cow to help.

☐ 1 mark

5 Then a _____ mouse came to help.

☐ 1 mark

Challenge 2

1 Write numbers in the boxes to show the order of events in the story. One has been done for you.

The little mouse came to help.	
The old woman wanted to cook turnip soup.	
They got the cow to help.	
The dog tried to help.	
The cat joined in.	
She asked the old man to help.	2

☐ 1 mark

☐ 1 mark

☐ 1 mark

☐ 1 mark

☐ 1 mark

Challenge 3

Write answers to these questions.

1 Where did the old woman go to pull up a turnip?

....

2 Who was first to help the old woman?

....

3 Write the names of all the animals who tried to help.

....

....

4 What noise did the turnip make when it came out?

....

5 Which animal was the last to help the old woman?

....

6 What did they all shout when the turnip came out?

....

Total: _____ / 19 marks

😐 **Had a go** ☐   🙂 **Getting there** ☐   😄 **Got it!** ☐

Beans on Toast

You will need:

Bread

Butter

Beans

An adult to help you

Pan

Toaster

Knife

What to do:

Tip the beans into a pan and cook them.

Put the bread in the toaster and toast it.

Spread butter on the toast.

Pour the beans on top of the toast.

Your beans on toast is now ready to eat!

Challenge 1

1 Label the three ingredients you need to make beans on toast.

BAKED BEAN

....

3 marks

2 What else do you need?

....

4 marks

Challenge 2

Write in the missing words.

1 Tip the .... into a pan and cook them.

1 mark

2 Put the bread in the .... and toast it.

1 mark

3 .... butter on the toast.

1 mark

4 Pour the beans on top of the ....

1 mark

Challenge 3

1 Number the instructions so they are in the right order.

Put the bread in the toaster and toast it. ☐   ☐ 1 mark

Pour the beans on top of the toast. ☐   ☐ 1 mark

Tip the beans into a pan and cook them. ☐   ☐ 1 mark

Spread butter on the toast. ☐   ☐ 1 mark

2 Here are some more ingredients:

grated cheese   **ketchup**   **salt and pepper**

Choose one of the ingredients. Write a sentence to show how you would add it to the beans on toast.

....

....

....
☐ 1 mark

Total: _____ / 16 marks

😐 **Had a go** ☐   🙂 **Getting there** ☐   😄 **Got it!** ☐

Five Little Owls

Five little owls in an old elm tree,

Fluffy and puffy as owls could be,

Blinking and winking with big round eyes

At the big round moon that hung in the skies:

As I passed beneath I could hear one say,

'There'll be mouse for supper, there will, today!'

Then all of them hooted, 'Tu-whit, Tu-whoo.

Yes, mouse for supper, Hoo hoo, hoo hoo!'

Anon

Challenge 1

Write in the missing words.

1 Five little _____ in an old elm tree.

2 Fluffy and _____ as owls could be.

3 Blinking and winking with big _____ eyes.

4 At the big round _____ that hung in the skies.

5 Then all of them _____, 'Tu-whit, Tu-whoo.

6 Yes, mouse for _____, Hoo hoo, hoo hoo!'

Challenge 2

1 Draw lines to match the rhyming words.

tree	today
eyes	be
say	hoo
Tu-whoo	skies

Challenge 3

1 Tick to show whether each statement is **True** or **False**.

	True	False	
The title of the poem is 'Five Little Owls'.			1 mark
The owls are sitting in an elm tree.			1 mark
The owls have big round eyes.			1 mark
The owls are going to have fish to eat.			1 mark
The sun is in the sky.			1 mark

Total: _____ / 15 marks

😐 **Had a go** ☐   🙂 **Getting there** ☐   😃 **Got it!** ☐

At the Beach

Abdu and Gem had waited all week to go to the seaside.
Now it was Saturday, it was time to go.

Gem's Nan put their bags in the car and off they went.

First, they put on their swimming costumes and raced into the sea.

Then they got their buckets and spades. They built a huge sandcastle.

Nan had made a picnic for lunch.
They ate sandwiches and cake and drank cool lemon squash.

They played with their kite and had a donkey ride.

Abdu got an ice cream and Gem got a red lolly.

Nan said it was time to go home.

Abdu and Gem fell asleep in the car.

Challenge 1

Tick the correct answer.

1 How long had Abdu and Gem waited to go to the seaside?

All month ☐   **All day** ☐   **All week** ☐   ☐ I mark

2 Which day did Abdu and Gem go to the seaside?

Monday ☐   **Friday** ☐   **Saturday** ☐   ☐ I mark

3 How did Abdu and Gem get to the seaside?

in a car ☐   **on a train** ☐   **on a bus** ☐   ☐ I mark

4 What did Abdu and Gem do after they'd put on their swimming costumes?

Go in the sea ☐   **Build a sandcastle** ☐

Have a picnic ☐   ☐ I mark

5 Who had made a picnic?

Abdu ☐   **Gem** ☐   **Nan** ☐   ☐ I mark

6 What flavour was the squash?

blackcurrant ☐   **lemon** ☐   **lime** ☐   ☐ I mark

7 What animal did Abdu and Gem ride?

donkey ☐   **horse** ☐   **pony** ☐   ☐ I mark

8 Who took Abdu and Gem to the seaside?

Mum ☐   **Dad** ☐   **Nan** ☐   ☐ I mark

Challenge 2

Answer these questions.

1 How long had Abdu and Gem waited to go to the seaside?

....

1 mark

2 What did Nan put in the car? ....

1 mark

3 What did they use to build the sandcastle?

.... and ....

2 marks

4 What did they have for lunch? ....

....

3 marks

5 Who had a red lolly? ....

1 mark

Challenge 3

1 Write numbers in the boxes to show the order of events in the story. One has been done for you.

Nan said it was time to go home.	5
They had a picnic for lunch.	
They put on their swimming costumes.	
They fell asleep in the car.	
Nan put their bags in the car.	
They played with their kite.	

1 mark

1 mark

1 mark

1 mark

1 mark

Total: _____ / 21 marks

😐 **Had a go** ☐   🙂 **Getting there** ☐   😃 **Got it!** ☐

39

Polar Bears

Daria Krakov

Table of Contents

Challenge 1

1 What is the title of the book? ....
[ ] 1 mark

2 What is the name of the author? ....
[ ] 1 mark

3 Where would you expect to find the Table of Contents?
....
[ ] 1 mark

4 Fill in the missing page numbers and chapter headings in this copy of the table of contents.

Who Am I?	4
	6
Powerful Paws	
	12
	14
Bears in Town	
7 Amazing Polar Bear Facts	
Cute Cubs	
	28
What in the World?	
Glossary	32

[ ] 1 mark
[ ] 1 mark
[ ] 1 mark
[ ] 1 mark
[ ] 1 mark
[ ] 1 mark
[ ] 1 mark
[ ] 1 mark
[ ] 1 mark

Challenge 2

1 Tick to show whether each statement is **True** or **False**.

	True	False	
The title of the book is *Bears*.			1 mark
The book is written by Daria Krakov.			1 mark
The book is a fiction book.			1 mark
There is information in the book about how polar bears play.			1 mark

Challenge 3

Answer these questions.

1 What does the contents page tell you about the size of polar bears? ....
1 mark

2 Which word tells you that polar bears have strong paws?

....
1 mark

3 What is the title of the chapter where you would find out about what polar bears eat?

....
1 mark

4 Are polar bears good at swimming? ....
1 mark

5 What makes you think this?

....
1 mark

Total: _____ / 21 marks

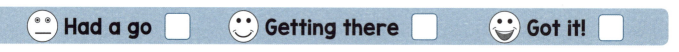

😐 Had a go ☐   🙂 Getting there ☐   😃 Got it! ☐

42

Little Boy Blue

Little Boy Blue,
Come blow your horn,
The sheep's in the meadow,
The cow's in the corn.
Where is the boy
Who looks after the sheep?
He's under a haystack
Fast asleep.
Will you wake him?
No, not I,
For if I do,
He's sure to cry.

Challenge 1

1 Draw lines to match the rhyming words.

horn	cry
sheep	corn
I	asleep

1 mark

1 mark

1 mark

2 Think of a word that rhymes with each of these words from the poem.

boy ....

blue ....

wake ....

3 marks

Challenge 2

1 Tick to show whether each statement is **True** or **False**.

	True	False
The sheep's in the meadow.		
The cow's in the haystack.		
The boy is in the corn.		
The boy will cry if he's woken up.		

1 mark

1 mark

1 mark

1 mark

Challenge 3

Answer these questions.

1 What is the boy asked to blow?

....

I mark

2 What animal is in the meadow?

....

I mark

3 Where is the cow?

....

I mark

4 What is the boy's job?

....

I mark

5 Where is the boy?

....

I mark

6 Why might Little Boy Blue have fallen asleep?

....

I mark

Total: _____ / 16 marks

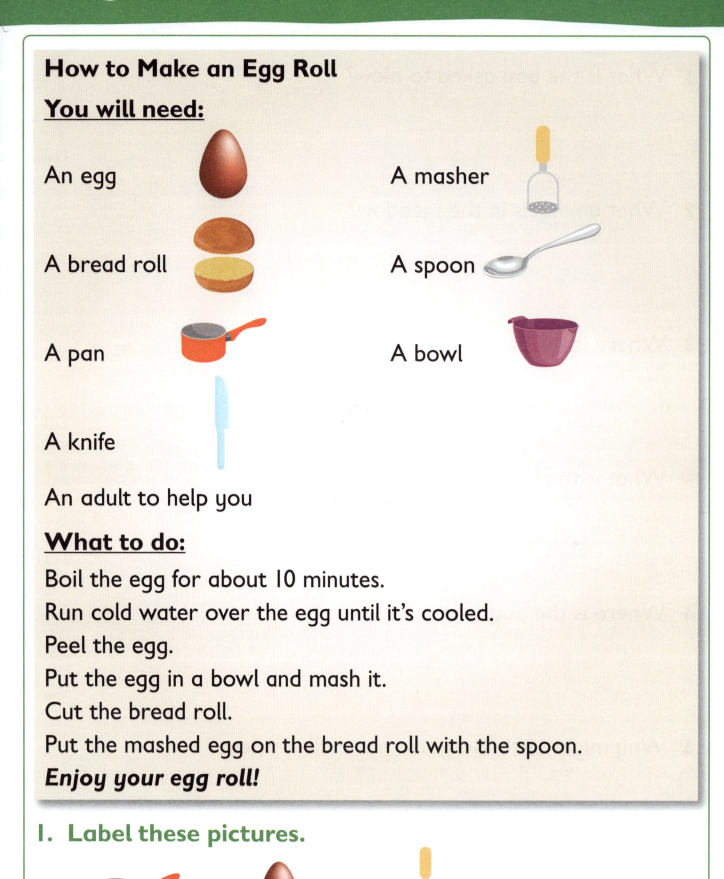

How to Make an Egg Roll

You will need:

An egg

A bread roll

A pan

A knife

A masher

A spoon

A bowl

An adult to help you

What to do:

Boil the egg for about 10 minutes.
Run cold water over the egg until it's cooled.
Peel the egg.
Put the egg in a bowl and mash it.
Cut the bread roll.
Put the mashed egg on the bread roll with the spoon.
Enjoy your egg roll!

1. **Label these pictures.**

....

4 marks

2. **Write numbers in the boxes to put the instructions in the correct order. One has been done for you.**

Peel the egg.	
Boil the egg for about 10 minutes.	1
Cut the bread roll.	
Put the mashed egg on the bread roll with the spoon.	
Put the egg in a bowl and mash it.	
Run cold water over the egg until it's cooled.	

1 mark

1 mark

1 mark

1 mark

1 mark

Big Cats

Table of Contents

3. Fill in the missing page numbers and chapter headings in this copy of the table of contents.

Where in the world?	4
Meet the Big Cat family	
Cuddly cubs	12
Sharp teeth and claws	
	16
Big Cats at play	18
Are Big Cats like your cat at home?	
	22
Glossary	24

1 mark

1 mark

1 mark

1 mark

1 mark

Answer these questions about the table of contents.

4. What is the title of the book? ....

1 mark

5. Which page would you read to find out where in the world Big Cats live? ....

1 mark

6. What type of Big Cats are described as cuddly?

....

1 mark

7. What will you read about on page 14?

....

1 mark

Hey Diddle Diddle

Hey diddle diddle,

The cat and the fiddle,

The cow jumped over the moon;

The little dog laughed to see such fun,

And the dish ran away with the spoon.

Tick to show the correct answers.

8. **How many lines are there in the poem?**

five ☐   six ☐

9. **Which word rhymes with diddle?**

fun ☐   fiddle ☐

10. **Which word rhymes with moon?**

diddle ☐   spoon ☐

11. **Who jumped over the moon?**

the cow ☐   the cat ☐

12. **Who laughed to see such fun?**

the spoon ☐   the dog ☐

13. **Who ran away with the spoon?**

the dish ☐   the fiddle ☐

Total: _____ / 24 marks

My Old Teddy

My old Teddy's leg came off.

Poor old Teddy!

I took him to the Teddy doctor.

She made Teddy better.

My old Teddy's arm came off.

Poor old Teddy!

I took him to the Teddy doctor.

She made Teddy better.

My old Teddy's ear came off.

Poor old Teddy!

I took him to the Teddy doctor.

She made Teddy better.

Then poor old Teddy's head came off.

The Teddy doctor said Teddy's had enough now…

Teddy had to rest.

The Teddy doctor gave me…

my new Teddy.

I love new Teddy very much, but I love poor old Teddy best.

Dear old, poor old Teddy.

By Dom Mansell

Challenge 1

Write the missing words in the sentences.

1 My old _____ leg came off.

1 mark

2 I took him to the Teddy _____ .

1 mark

3 My _____ Teddy's arm came off.

1 mark

4 The Teddy doctor _____ Teddy's had enough now…

1 mark

5 I _____ new Teddy very much,

but I _____ poor old Teddy best.

2 marks

Challenge 2

1 Write numbers in the boxes to show the order of events in the story. One has been done for you.

Teddy had to rest.	
Teddy's leg came off.	1
Teddy's head came off.	
Teddy's ear came off.	
Teddy's arm came off.	

1 mark

1 mark

1 mark

1 mark

52

1 Tick to show whether each statement is **True** or **False**.

	True	False	
Teddy was made better by the dentist.			1 mark
Teddy's arm could not be mended.			1 mark
Old Teddy had to rest.			1 mark
The narrator loves old Teddy more than new Teddy.			1 mark

2 Do you think a child or a grown-up is narrating the story?

....

1 mark

3 What makes you think this?

....

1 mark

4 Find and copy some words that show the narrator liked Teddy very much.

....

1 mark

5 Do you have a teddy?   Yes / No
How do you feel about your teddy?

....

2 marks

Total: _____ / 19 marks

Blackbirds

Blackbirds are very common birds that like to live in gardens and parks.

Male blackbirds have glossy black feathers and bright yellow beaks. They also have a yellow ring around their eyes and brownish-black legs.

Female blackbirds have dark brown feathers. Young blackbirds are also brown with lighter brown spots on their chest.

Blackbirds eat lots of different food including insects, berries and fruit. They also like to pull worms out of the ground for a tasty treat.

Blackbirds build nests in trees and bushes. Female blackbirds lay between three and five tiny blue eggs in these nests. They sit on the eggs to keep them warm until they hatch.

When the eggs hatch, both parents feed the baby blackbirds with worms and other food.

When they are big enough, the baby blackbirds leave the nest and learn to catch their own food.

1 Label the picture of the blackbird. Use the words from the text to help you write detailed labels.

4 marks

Challenge 2

1 Tick to show whether each statement is **True** or **False**.

	True	False
Female blackbirds are brown.		
Blackbirds lay brown eggs.		
Blackbirds build nests in flowerpots.		
Blackbirds lay between three and five eggs.		

1 mark

1 mark

1 mark

1 mark

Challenge 3

Answer these questions.

1 Male blackbirds have glossy black feathers. What is another
word with a similar meaning to glossy? .... [ ]
1 mark

2 What colour is a male blackbird's beak? .... [ ]
1 mark

3 Where do blackbirds build their nests? ....

.... [ ]
2 marks

4 What colour are young blackbirds? .... [ ]
1 mark

5 What foods do blackbirds like to eat? ....

....

.... [ ]
4 marks

6 What do blackbird eggs look like? ....

.... [ ]
2 marks

Total: _____ / 19 marks

Cleaning Your Teeth

Every morning and every night,
Brush your teeth to keep them bright.

Squeeze some toothpaste on your brush,
Not too little, nor too much.

Turn the tap on. Wet your brush.
Start to clean, but do not rush.

Don't press too hard. Keep it light.
This will keep your smile all white.

To keep your teeth your whole life long,
Also brush your gums and tongue.

Two minutes brushing, front and back,
Will keep your teeth from going black.

When you've finished, take a drink.
Spit the water in the sink.

Challenge 1

1 Draw lines to match the rhyming words.

night	rush
brush	sink
back	bright
drink	black

1 mark

1 mark

1 mark

1 mark

2 Think of a word that rhymes with each of these words:

Night ....

Brush ....

Long ....

Black ....

Drink ....

5 marks

Challenge 2

1 Write numbers in the boxes to show the order of events in the poem. One has been done for you.

When you've finished, take a drink.	6
Don't press too hard.	
Also brush your gums and tongue.	
Turn the tap on.	
Squeeze some toothpaste on your brush.	
Two minutes brushing, front and back.	

1 mark

1 mark

1 mark

1 mark

1 mark

Challenge 3

1 Tick to show whether each statement is **True** or **False**.

	True	False	
You should brush your teeth every morning and every night.			I mark
You should put lots of toothpaste on your toothbrush.			I mark
You should rush and brush your teeth quickly.			I mark
You should brush your gums and tongue.			I mark
You should brush your teeth for two minutes.			I mark

2 What should you squeeze onto your toothbrush?

....

I mark

3 What might happen if you rush when you brush your teeth?

....

I mark

4 Why do you think you shouldn't press too hard when you

brush your teeth? ....

I mark

5 What would happen if you don't brush your teeth?

....

I mark

Total: _____ / 23 marks

Goldilocks and the Three Bears

There were once three bears who lived in a cottage in the woods.

They were Daddy Bear and Mummy Bear who were both big and gruff. And Baby Bear who was very small.

Each morning, they had porridge for breakfast. One day it was too hot to eat so they went for a walk while it cooled.

While they were away, a little girl called Goldilocks crept into their cottage. She was hungry so she tried the bears' porridge. Daddy Bear's porridge was too hot. Mummy Bear's porridge was too cold. But Baby Bear's porridge was just right so she ate it all up.

Goldilocks now wanted to sit down. She looked at Daddy Bear's chair but it was too high and she couldn't get onto it. Mummy Bear's chair was too hard. So she tried Baby Bear's chair. It felt just right. But she was too heavy. The chair broke!

Goldilocks yawned. She went upstairs and tried the three bears' beds. Daddy Bear's bed was too soft. Mummy Bear's bed had too many pillows and Goldilocks couldn't get comfy. Baby Bear's bed was just right and she fell asleep.

Soon the three bears came home. Baby Bear saw the problem right away. He ran through the cottage and shouted to Daddy and Mummy Bear, 'Someone's eaten my porridge and broken my chair AND THEY ARE ASLEEP IN MY BED!'

Daddy Bear and Mummy Bear were very, very cross. They growled very, very loudly.

Goldilocks woke up and ran away as fast as she could.

What a naughty girl!

Challenge 1

Write the missing words in the sentences.

1 There were once three _____ who lived in a cottage in the woods.

2 Each morning, they had porridge for

_____ .

1 mark

3 While they were away, a little girl called Goldilocks

_____ into their cottage.

1 mark

4 She went _____ and tried the three bears' beds.

1 mark

5 Daddy Bear and Mummy Bear were very,

very _____ .

1 mark

6 Goldilocks woke up and ran away as

_____ as she could.

1 mark

Challenge 2

Answer these questions.

1 What type of home did the three bears live in?

_____

1 mark

2 Why did the three bears go for a walk?

_____

1 mark

3 Which word in the story shows that Goldilocks was tired?

_____

1 mark

4 How do you think Goldilocks felt when Daddy Bear and Mummy Bear growled?

....

1 mark

5 What makes you think this?

....

1 mark

Challenge 3

1 Use the story to help you complete the table.

	Porridge	Chair	Bed
Daddy Bear		Too high	Too soft
	Too cold		Too many pillows
Baby Bear			

1 mark

2 marks

3 marks

Total: _____ / 17 marks

Incredible Insects: Butterflies

Nature is full of fantastic animals that do amazing things. Butterflies are one of the best. During their life, they make the most amazing changes. They are truly incredible insects!

There are four stages in the lifecycle of a butterfly.

Stage 1 – egg

A female butterfly lays tiny round eggs on a leaf.

Stage 2 – larva

An egg hatches and a butterfly **larva** pops out. We call the larva a caterpillar.

Caterpillars are VERY hungry. They eat a lot and they grow a lot too.

Stage 3 – pupa

When a caterpillar has stopped growing, it forms itself into a **pupa**. We sometimes call the pupa a **chrysalis**. The caterpillar looks like it is wrapped up asleep, but inside the chrysalis, it is busy **transforming**.

Stage 4 – adult

When the caterpillar has finished transforming, it breaks out of the chrysalis. It now has wings and six legs. It is a butterfly.

Its wings are wet to start with so it needs to let them dry. After a short rest, it's soon ready to fly off. The lifecycle is ready to begin again.

Glossary

chrysalis – the name sometimes given to a caterpillar in the stage between being a larva and being an adult

larva – the name of an insect before it becomes an adult

pupa – another name for a chrysalis

transforming – changing from one thing into another thing

Challenge 1

1 Number each stage to show the order it comes in the text. One has been done for you.

larva	
butterfly	4
egg	
pupa	

1 mark

1 mark

1 mark

Challenge 2

Write the missing words in these sentences from the text.

1 There are .... stages in the lifecycle of a butterfly.

1 mark

2 A .... butterfly lays tiny round eggs on a leaf.

1 mark

3 Caterpillars are VERY ....

1 mark

4 When a caterpillar has stopped ...., it forms itself into a pupa.

1 mark

5 It now has .... and six legs.

1 mark

6 Its wings are .... to start with so it needs to let them dry.

1 mark

7 The .... is ready to begin again.

1 mark

Challenge 3

Write answers to these questions. Use the text to help you.

1 What type of animal is a butterfly? .... ☐ 1 mark

2 What do we call a larva? .... ☐ 1 mark

3 Do you think the author likes butterflies? .... ☐ 1 mark

4 Write a word from the text that makes you think this.

.... ☐ 1 mark

5 Why do you think there is a glossary in this text?

.... ☐ 1 mark

6 What do you think caterpillars eat? .... ☐ 1 mark

7 What does it look like the caterpillar is doing when it

forms a pupa? .... ☐ 1 mark

8 What word is used in the text that means 'changing from

one thing into another thing'? .... ☐ 1 mark

Total: _____ / 18 marks

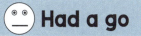 **Had a go** ☐   **Getting there** ☐    **Got it!** ☐

Progress Test 3

Sammy's Lunch

Sammy had left his lunch at home. He started to cry.

'Don't worry,' said Mo. 'I have two sandwiches. You can have one of them.'

'Thank you,' said Sammy.

'I have three slices of cake,' said Meena. 'I can't eat them all. You can have one of them.'

'Thank you,' said Sammy.

'I have a big bunch of grapes,' said Geeta. 'You can have some of them.'

'Thank you,' said Sammy.

'I have a spare carton of juice,' said Mrs Green. 'You can have that.'

'Thank you everyone,' said Sammy. 'This is the best lunch ever!'

Tick to show the correct answers.

1. **Where did Sammy leave his lunch?**

   at home ☐   on the bus ☐   in the car ☐   ☐

   1 mark

2. **What are the names of the children in the story?**

   Kaylee ☐   Sammy ☐   Mo ☐

   Meena ☐   Rizwan ☐   Geeta ☐   ☐

   4 marks

3. What did Sammy have for lunch in the end?

an apple ☐   a sandwich ☐   a yoghurt ☐

some crisps ☐   some nuts ☐   some grapes ☐

some cheese ☐   a carton of juice ☐   a slice of cake ☐

☐ 4 marks

4. Write numbers in the boxes to show the order of events in the story. One has been done for you.

Meena said he could have a slice of her cake.	
Geeta shared her grapes with Sammy.	
Mrs Green gave Sammy a carton of juice.	5
Sammy had left his lunch at home.	
Mo gave him a sandwich.	

☐ I mark
☐ I mark
☐ I mark
☐ I mark

Answer these questions about the story.

5. How do you think Sammy felt at the beginning of the story? ....

☐ I mark

6. What makes you think this? ....

☐ I mark

7. How many sandwiches did Mo have? ....

☐ I mark

8. How many slices of cake did Meena have? ....

☐ I mark

9. What did Geeta share with Sammy? ....

☐ I mark

10. What did Mrs Green give to Sammy?

☐ I mark

Robins

Robins are friendly little birds. They are easy to spot because of their bright red faces and tummies.

When a pair of robins are ready to have babies, the female builds a tiny nest.

Robins build their nests near to the ground in bushes, hedges and piles of logs.

Robins sometimes build their nests in unusual places such as plant pots, garden sheds and even in wellies!

When the nest has been built, the female robin lays between four and six tiny eggs. She sits on the eggs to keep them warm. The male robin catches food for her to eat.

After 13 days, the eggs hatch.

The robin chicks stay in the nest for two weeks where they are fed and looked after by their parents.

After this, they learn how to fly. Then they leave the nest and catch their own food. The male robin looks after them until they are ready to look after themselves.

Write the missing words in these sentences from the text.

11. **Robins are friendly** .... **birds.**

1 mark

12. **They are easy to spot because of their bright**
     .... **faces and tummies.**

1 mark

13. **Robins build their** .... **near to the ground in bushes, hedges and piles of logs.**

1 mark

14. She sits on the eggs to keep them ....

1 mark

15. After 13 days, the .... hatch.

1 mark

16. Tick to show whether each statement is **True** or **False**.

	True	False
Robins are unfriendly birds.		
The male robin builds the nest.		
Robins sometimes build their nests in plant pots.		
The female robin lays between four and six tiny eggs.		
The eggs hatch after 13 days.		
The chicks stay in the nest for three weeks.		

1 mark

1 mark

1 mark

1 mark

1 mark

1 mark

Reread the text and use it to help you answer these questions.

17. **Can you write two places where robins build their nests?** ....

2 marks

18. **Can you write two things that the female robin does on her own?** ....

2 marks

19. **Which thing do the male and female do together?**

....

1 mark

20. **Which two things does the male robin do on his own?** ....

2 marks

Total: _____ / 37 marks

Answers

Pages 6–11 Starter Test

1. pan, penguin [2]
2. Make sure your child has correctly written the two words. [2]
3. tin, tap [2]
4. Make sure your child has correctly written the two words. [2]
5. pit, nip, sit, tip, nit, sip [6]
6. pan, nap, sap, tan [4]
7. 2, 1, 3 [3]
8. tick, tock, pack, kick, sock clock, quack, dock, chick, back [10]
9. Dock, clock, down, Dock [4]
10. Make sure your child has read and pointed to all the words. [8]
11. sea, sand, starfish [3]
12. ball, bucket, beach [3]
13. beach, six children, two buckets, on the sand, in the sea [5]
14. Make sure your child has read all the words. [6]
15. hen, duck, cat, dog, cow, bee [6]
16. Cows go moo!
    The hen laid an egg.
    The dog has a long tail. [3]
17. 2, 1, 4, 3 [4]
18. Jill, hill, fell, well [4]
19. Jill, hill, fell [3]
20. down, crown, owl, now [4]
21. Make sure your child has read and pointed to all the words. [5]
22. at school, eight children, on the stool, in the box [4]
23. book, blocks, hat [3]

Pages 12–13

Challenge 1

1. box, teddy, moon, boots [4]

Challenge 2

1. rug [1]
2. higher [1]
3. teddy, picnic [2]
4. box [1]

Challenge 3

1. a rocket [1]
2. a pink bun [1]
3. he put it away [1]
4. Child's own answer. [1]

Pages 14–15

Challenge 1

1. cub [1]
2. vixen [1]
3. den [1]

Challenge 2

1. One mark for each correct label: red coat, bushy tail, long snout, long legs, pointed ears [5]

Challenge 3

1. at night [1]
2. rubbish and meat [2]
3. in the day [1]

Pages 16–17

Challenge 1

1. seagulls [1]
2. the shops [1]
3. the playground [1]
4. animals [1]

Challenge 2

1. screech [1]
2. at the park [1]
3. at the swimming pool [1]

Challenge 3

1. moo, baa, oink [3]

Pages 18–19

Challenge 1

1. happy [1]
2. nest [1]
3. best [1]
4. eggs [1]

Challenge 2

1. happy [1]
2. four [1]
3. sat [1]

Challenge 3

1. tip, top, tap [3]
2. beaks / four little beaks [1]
3. four [1]

Pages 20–21

Challenge 1

1. elephant, frog, rabbit, cat [4]

Challenge 2

1. inside its head [1]
2. long and thin [1]
3. furry [1]

Challenge 3

1. us / we do / people / children / humans [1]
2. To keep cool [1]
3. 1 mark per animal, 1 mark per description of ears [6]

Pages 22–23

Challenge 1

1. sitting [1]
2. yak [1]
3. fish [1]
4. socks [1]

Challenge 2

1. eye [1]
2. muffin [1]
3. mac [1]
4. wish [1]

Challenge 3

1. man, tan, van [3]
2. fair (fare), chair, stair (stare) [3]
3. dog, fog (frog), cog [3]

Pages 24–27 Progress Test 1

1. One mark for each correct label: hood, pockets, zip [3]
2. Make sure your child has coloured the picture of the coat in red. [1]
3. Rex [1]
4. brown [1]
4. big [1]
6. meat [1]
7. ball [1]
8. little [1]
9. handle [1]
10. Here [1]
11. steamed [1]
12. pour [1]
13. toes, nails [2]
14. pads, claws [2]
14. pads [1]
15. cats [1]

Pages 28–30

Challenge 1

1. cook [1]
2. stuck [1]
3. held [1]
4. got [1]
5. little [1]

Challenge 2

The little mouse came to help.	6
The old woman wanted to cook turnip soup.	1
They got the cow to help.	3
The dog tried to help.	4
The cat joined in.	5
She asked the old man to help.	2

[5]

Challenge 3

1. the garden [1]
2. the old man [1]
3. cow, dog, cat, mouse [4]
4. POP! [1]
5. the mouse [1]
6. Hooray! [1]

Pages 31–33

Challenge 1

1. bread, butter, beans [3]
2. pan, toaster, knife, adult [4]

Challenge 2

1. beans [1]
2. toaster [1]
3. Spread [1]
4. toast [1]

Challenge 3

1. 2, 4, 1, 3 [4]
2. Child's own answer. [1]

Pages 34–36

Challenge 1

1. owls [1]
2. puffy [1]
3. round [1]
4. moon [1]
5. hooted [1]
6. supper [1]

Challenge 2

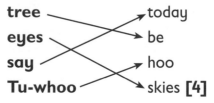

tree — today
eyes — be
say — hoo
Tu-whoo — skies [4]

Challenge 3

1. True [1]
2. True [1]
3. True [1]
4. False [1]
5. False [1]

Pages 37–39

Challenge 1

1. All week [1]
2. Saturday [1]
3. in a car [1]
4. Go in the sea [1]
5. Nan [1]
6. lemon [1]
7. donkey [1]
8. Nan [1]

Challenge 2

1. all week [1]
2. their bags [1]
3. buckets and spades [2]
4. sandwiches, cake, lemon squash [3]
5. Gem [1]

Challenge 3

1.

Nan said it was time to go home.	5
They had a picnic for lunch.	3
They put on their swimming costumes.	2
They fell asleep in the car.	6
Nan put their bags in the car.	1
They played with their kite.	4

[5]

Pages 40–42

Challenge 1

1. Polar Bears' [1]
2. Daria Krakov [1]
3. at the front of the book [1]
4.

Who Am I?	4	
Big Bears!	6	
Powerful Paws	**10**	
Super Swimmers	12	
What's for Dinner?	14	
Bears in Town	**20**	
7 Amazing Polar Bear Facts	**22**	
Cute Cubs	**24**	
Playtime!	28	
What in the World?	**30**	
Glossary	32	**[9]**

Challenge 2

1. False, True, False, True [4]

Challenge 3

1. They are big [1]
2. Powerful [1]
3. What's for Dinner? [1]
4. Yes [1]
5. There is a chapter called 'Super Swimmers' [1]

Pages 43–45

Challenge 1

1. horn — cry
   sheep — corn
   I — asleep [3]
2. Any rhyming words, e.g. toy, shoe, cake [3]

Challenge 2

1. True, False, False, True [4]

Challenge 3

1. his horn [1]
2. the sheep [1]
3. in the corn [1]
4. to look after the sheep [1]
5. under a haystack [1]
6. Child's own answer, e.g. he might have worked hard; he might be tired from working; it was sunny which made him sleepy. [1]

Pages 46–49 Progress Test 2

1. pan, egg, masher, spoon [4]
2.

Peel the egg.	3	
Boil the egg for about 10 minutes.	1	
Cut the bread roll.	5	
Put the mashed egg on the bread roll with the spoon.	6	
Put the egg in a bowl and mash it.	4	
Run cold water over the egg until it's cooled.	2	**[5]**

3.

Where in the world?	4	
Meet the Big Cat family	6	
Cuddly cubs	12	
Sharp teeth and claws	**14**	
It's meat for dinner!	16	
Big Cats at play	18	
Are Big Cats like your cat at home?	**20**	
Ten cool facts about Big Cats	22	
Glossary	24	**[5]**

4. Big Cats [1]
5. 4 [1]
6. Cubs [1]
7. Sharp teeth and claws [1]
8. five [1]
9. fiddle [1]
10. spoon [1]
11. the cow [1]
12. the dog [1]
13. the dish [1]

Pages 50–53

Challenge 1

1. Teddy's **[1]**
2. doctor **[1]**
3. old **[1]**
4. said **[1]**
5. love, love **[2]**

Challenge 2

1.

Teddy had to rest.	5
Teddy's leg came off.	1
Teddy's head came off.	4
Teddy's ear came off.	3
Teddy's arm came off.	2

[4]

Challenge 3

1. False, False, True, True **[4]**
2. a child **[1]**
3. Grown-ups don't tend to have a teddy. **[1]**
4. 'I love poor old Teddy best.' **[1]**
5. Child's own answer **[2]**

Pages 54–57

Challenge 1

1. One mark for each correct label: black (or brown) feathers, yellow beak, yellow ring around eye, brownish-black legs **[4]**

Challenge 2

1. True, False, False, True **[4]**

Challenge 3

1. Accept any word with a similar meaning to glossy, e.g. shiny. **[1]**
2. yellow / bright yellow **[1]**
3. in trees and bushes **[2]**
4. Brown **[1]**
5. Insects, berries, fruit and worms **[4]**
6. Tiny and blue **[2]**

Pages 58–61

Challenge 1

1.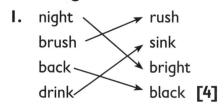

   night → bright
   brush → sink
   back → rush
   drink → black **[4]**

2. Accept any suitable rhyming words. **[5]**

Challenge 2

1.

When you've finished, take a drink.	6
Don't press too hard.	3
Also brush your gums and tongue.	4
Turn the tap on.	2
Squeeze some toothpaste on your brush.	1
Two minutes brushing, front and back.	5

[5]

Challenge 3

1. True, False, False, True, True **[5]**
2. toothpaste **[1]**
3. You might not do it properly/you might miss some of your teeth out. **[1]**
4. You might hurt your gums/you might cause some damage. **[1]**
5. They might decay/go black/become bad/diseased. **[1]**

Pages 62–65

Challenge 1

1. bears **[1]**
2. breakfast **[1]**
3. crept **[1]**
4. upstairs **[1]**
5. cross **[1]**
6. fast **[1]**

Challenge 2

1. a cottage **[1]**
2. to let their porridge cool down / because their porridge was too hot **[1]**

3. yawned **[1]**

4. frightened / scared **[1]**

5. Child's own answer, e.g., she ran away; the growl was loud **[1]**

Challenge 3

1.

	Porridge	**Chair**	**Bed**
Daddy Bear	**Too hot**	Too high	Too soft
Mummy Bear	Too cold	**Too hard**	Too many pillows
Baby Bear	**Just right**	**Just right**	**Just right**

[6]

Pages 66–69

Challenge 1

1.

larva	2
butterfly	4
egg	1
pupa	3

[3]

Challenge 2

1. four **[1]**

2. female **[1]**

3. hungry **[1]**

4. growing **[1]**

5. wings **[1]**

6. wet **[1]**

7. lifecycle **[1]**

Challenge 3

1. insect **[1]**

2. a caterpillar **[1]**

3. yes **[1]**

4. Any from: fantastic, amazing, best, incredible. **[1]**

5. there are lots of words you may not know **[1]**

6. leaves (there is a clue in the image) **[1]**

7. sleeping **[1]**

8. transforming **[1]**

Pages 70–73 Progress Test 3

1. at home **[1]**

2. Sammy, Mo, Meena, Geeta **[4]**

3. a sandwich, some grapes, a carton of juice, a slice of cake **[4]**

4.

Meena said he could have a slice of her cake.	3
Geeta shared her grapes with Sammy.	4
Mrs Green gave Sammy a carton of juice.	5
Sammy had left his lunch at home.	1
Mo gave him a sandwich.	2

[4]

5. sad / unhappy (accept hungry) **[1]**

6. he started to cry (accept he didn't have any lunch) **[1]**

7. two **[1]**

8. three **[1]**

9. grapes **[1]**

10. a carton of juice **[1]**

11. little **[1]**

12. red **[1]**

13. nests **[1]**

14. warm **[1]**

15. eggs **[1]**

16. False, False, True, True, True, False **[6]**

17. Any two from: bushes, hedges, piles of logs, plant pots, garden sheds, wellies. **[2]**

18. Any two from: builds the nest, lays the eggs, sits on the eggs. **[2]**

19. Feed the chicks / look after the chicks **[1]**

20. Feeds the female, looks after the fledglings / young robins **[2]**

Fill in your score for each progress test in the window of the rocket.

Progress Test 1

Progress Test 2

Progress Test 3